SKETCHES/RIO DE JANEIRO

& OTHER POEMS

poems by

Arthur Powers

Finishing Line Press
Georgetown, Kentucky

SKETCHES/RIO DE JANEIRO

& OTHER POEMS

Publisher: Leah Maines

Editor: Christen Kincaid

Cover Art: Photo by Robert Nyman on Unsplash

Author Photo: Caroline Flores-Powers

Cover Design: Elizabeth Maines McCleavy

Printed in the USA on acid-free paper.
Order online: www.finishinglinepress.com
            also available on amazon.com

Author inquiries and mail orders:
Finishing Line Press
P. O. Box 1626
Georgetown, Kentucky 40324
U. S. A.

Table of Contents

V. Tropical Thoughts

VI. Drylands: The Brazilian Northeast

VII. Rivers: The Brazilian Amazon

VIII. Wednesday Morning

for Brenda

Note on the text

In 1969, the author went to Brazil as a Peace Corps community organizer; he lived most of his adult life there. In the late 1970s, he practiced international law in Rio de Janeiro while his wife worked as a community organizer in the slums; they became aware of such things as—his clients paid more to stay one night in the big hotels in Copacabana than the chamber maids earned in a month. In 1985, he and his wife began work with the Catholic Church in the Amazon, organizing rural workers' unions and community groups in an area of violent land conflict. They lived with their two daughters in a village on the Araguaia River that had only one telephone (at the village telephone post) and electricity for only a few hours a day (& only when the village generator was working). Their lives were frequently threatened. After seven years, they moved to the drought-ridden Brazilian Northeast, where they worked on relief and development programs. In 1997 they returned to Rio de Janeiro.

This is the context that gave birth to these poems.

I

Daughters

A Mulata Child on the Itaipu Bus

At three years old, she is already
beautiful: the perfectly shaped lips
that pout, the gold earrings in pierced ears,
the long lashes and eyes that promise

deep hidden love. She has been crying:
hunger or sadness or fear has left
her cheeks marked wet, her hand tightly clenched,
her eyes brightly hurting to the sun.

Men born poor live by their wits, women
by their beauty. And who has neither
is bound in wheels of pain circled
by muscle and sweat and hard cut stone.

This is law. Yet the morning's glow
lies sweet and close, haloing her eyes.

Jardim Zoológico

(Rio de Janeiro, 1999)

There are cows at the zoo.
In a fenced area, next to the camels,
before the bend in the path that leads
by the cage with the big, black monkeys.
Ordinary cows and steers
such as one would see in any pasture.

The old people, stopping by the fence,
take a moment to recognize these beasts.
Straining their eyes to read the sign,
they look up bemused. Who would put cows
in a zoo? They chatter together, begin
to smile. One old man laughs.

Suddenly they are aware of their grandchildren
beside them, as rapt in cows as they were
in apes or elephants. The old people see that,
for these children, raised in tight apartments
and in the narrow paths of crowded slums,
getting milk from plastic sacks,

cows are as exotic as gazelles.
The old people's smiles falter.
They take their grandchildren's hands,
holding them with new fervor,
feeling the soft, malleable flesh
against their hardened palms.

Children's Story

(Rio de Janeiro)

The ships outside the bay,
white and gray, puffing smoke,
sit right on the horizon,
right on the line between
blue water and blue sky,
like ships in a child's drawing.

The ships wait on the horizon
because there are pirates
in the bay—not with black patches
and parrots on their shoulders,
but with semi-automatic pistols,
who board the ship and rob
and sometimes kill people.

The beach at Copacabana
is filled with bright umbrellas
—blue, green, yellow, red,
orange, purple—all mixed
with happy voices of people
talking, the crash of waves,
the ping of a beach ball.

At night on the beach
one does not walk
because men with knives
stalk in small bands
in order to rob people,
sometimes cutting them,
sometimes killing them.

The hills around the city
are dotted with bright
colored houses—pink
and white and blue.

Children fly kites
—orange and yellow—
from among the houses.

The hills are run
by drug gangs who
press small children
into running drugs.
They call them
"little airplanes"—
some children are hurt,
some are killed.

On the highest peak
a statue of Jesus stands,
arms outstretched in greeting
or in blessing.

My daughter says
his eyes are closed,
but I think they're open
and he sees
into all the hearts,
and in every heart
sees a little love,

even in pirates,
even in drug traffickers,
even in men with knives.

A Sidewalk on the Rua Rainha Elizabeth

(Rio de Janeiro, 2000)

The three-year-old girl
watches the men laying
the broad sidewalk that slopes
from the gas station to the street.

Cement flows from the truck's
rotating mixer. Two large men
hoe the cement into place,
then smooth it with a strong,

straight two-by-four. A small man
patches empty spots with a spatula,
then the big men with the board
smooth the cement again.

She watches, fascinated,
clinging to her mother's hand.
All her three-year life
she has seen sidewalks

but it never occurred to her
that someone makes them,
that they were not always there.

Twelve-Year-Old School Girls
Viewing Ancient Egyptian Coffins

(The Franco-Brazilian Exhibition,
Rio de Janeiro, March 3, 2002)

Dangling earrings, long black hair,
oval olive faces, bright black eyes,
lips made for murmuring rumors
("Do you know what *he* said *she* said?")

trying to listen as the female guide
instructs with clearly moving lips,
forming syllables of antique words
about the pretty painted patterns

of people so long dead, older
than parents, grandparents...
("Do you know what *she* said *he* said?")
striving (sort of) to understand,

while all along soul/body sings:
Alive, Alive, Alive, Alive!

Block Houses

(A hill above Botafogo, Rio de Janeiro)

Night. Electric light
flows from the open door.
My daughter builds block houses
on the patio tile.

One, two, three, four, five:
sharply visible in the light
that casts their shadows
on the polished tiles,

the small block houses
lie scattered in soft disorder
born not of logic
but in my daughter's beauty.

Each house is symmetrical,
perfectly rational in itself
and without apparent use.
And each is etched in color—

orange, yellow, blue, green, red:
bright roofs against startling pillars
and red thresholds where the light
more fully flows

building each house's shadow:
the smooth tile behind each
gleams black, and the black grows,
glowing and living,

on the garden bed,
brick wall, city roofs,
high on to where stars stand
naked in the sky.

Ana Cristina in Her Fourth Year

My daughter, when her heart is hurt,
is a lady. She stands erect,
her face turned delicate
as brown ivory, her perfect

skin transparent, her chin
and small ears quivering
to heart shaped lips, shivering
silence into the world's sin.

O her arms are straight and
held down and back at an angle
like a dancer's, while bird hands

flutter her fingers to spin
a world of wings as she angels
the day and lets all spirit in.

Angelica, at Ten Years of Age

She races across the garden
under the glaring tropical sun,
her dark black skin glistening.
She is the focal point, all colors run

behind her: blue sky, green leaves,
orange, yellow, purple flowers spun
in a whirlwind of whispering
relative to this girl, this one

so real being, center of swirl,
definite dark bright alive in the twirl
in which all is done and won.

Angelica in the Tropics

Dark flowing Arabic script
embossed on a white page:
so is my long, lithe, lovely daughter
against our sun blank days.

Skin ink black: smooth and soft
and glowing; and her ways
are supple, fluid, flexile letters
where holy writers trace

ornamental words of Allah
with a will as strong as rage:
so my daughter marks all matter
with her gentle grace.

II

Finding

Finding

(The Road to Castelo—Brazil 1971)

Down from the pine groves and granite
of the pass at Venda Nova, we take
the jeep along the twisting dirt road,
winding among hard gray fists of stone
outcropped from tight green pyramids
of mountain, Vadi beside me tensed
like a tendon, Zé Augusto in the back
rolling with the road, the air cold
on our windblown faces, headed toward
a place none of us knows, early morning
sky bright blue high above us, quiet
crisp clear day, until a certain turn,
a gentle wisp of warm air: far ahead
the road descends to distant palm trees
and the hills open slowly like a hand.

"Like White Swans Swimming, The Tropical Nuns..."

Like white swans swimming, the tropical nuns
glide on small steps in the warm night. They pass
on the street; their delicate chatter runs
ahead, tumbles behind, let out of mass.

Under the streetlamps small moons of light
catch their dark lively hands and faces
active with thought: startling against their white
habits. Laughing now, quickening their paces,

the flow home, excited minds in the calm
movement of white gowns—like sparkling bright
words in soft prayers, in ancient psalms.

In the Village of São Lourenço:
May, the Month of the Virgin (1969)

The electric lights dim, die. In the street
people pass like ghosts, except the laughs
of children dance down the dirt road. Half
way to the church we stop and meet
the new dark: there will be no feast
of the Virgin tonight. We turn,
descending, and watch the starlight burn
while candlelight patches drop in the dust
from stores.

          "How dead it is," she says
who has always lived here.

                        The ways
of the world are changing, my dear, and here
come the pretty, pious little girls
from church, dressed white as virgins, tiny, whirl-
ing home, their phantom faces bathed in tears.

In the Village of São Lourenço:
Portrait, with Distant Landscape (1969)

Celeste, who teaches planetary
science, walks down the dirt street, her black
thick hair waterfalling down her back,
her black sharp eyes staring airy-
thoughted at the sky.

                      Beyond the blue (which
is prism'd light) lies the black and end-
less interlocked with stars (Saturn and
Jupiter and Mars) and soon men will touch
the moon.

           The young boys watch her, and think her
pretty: they reach to catch her luster for
their memories. Higher, a cow browses
on a hill where grass plays in the wind,
and the road passes from Guaçui and
dips between two rows of plaster houses.

Poem in a White Room with a Window

--"As mangas que roubamos ficavam maduras."

"The mangos we stole have become ripe."
She reaches and picks one from the bowl by
the window. Her eyes find mine. Slowly
she lifts her hand to touch my lips
with quiet fingers.
                    And I am where
the wire fence ran along the dirt road;
the silent, dark-leafed mango trees glowed
in the sun; the light danced in her hair
and laughed.
                In the small, white room (the chair and
window frame painted blue) she lets her hand
drop and turns and looks out over the plain
to the hills in the west. The summer sky
trembles with a storm. Outside, nearby,
the wind rustling in the palms sounds like rain.

III

Sketches

Sketches/Rio de Janeiro

(The House Painter)

White paint speckling
dark blue pants and shirt,
dark brown skin,

his head capped
with a tall paper bag,

he stands
silent as a chieftain,
proud.

(The Peanut Girl)

Her eleven-year-old face
delicate blonde,
her one dress
always pressed,
she walks neatly
up and down
among the
open air restaurants

never smiling.

(The Beggar Woman)

She sits
on the black and white patterned
mosaic sidewalk in Copacabana,
her old legs like sticks
straight in front of her,

disdaining the crowd
that moves around her,
counting her money,
licking her thumb.

(The Housemaid)

Short and compact,
spilling energy like milk,
she scrubs and scrubs the morning
singing the kitchen clean.

(The Retired Judicial Clerk)

His old, feminine lips
sensuously form
meaningless whispers
behind his veined hands.

(The Pigeon Feeder)

He walks the plaza slowly,
haloed in white birds and bright daylight,
pouring gold grain from his bucket
into the sun.

(The Corporal)

His handsome face
notched and lined
like fine wood
from the forests
near his home
in the country,
he argues his point
steadily, steadily,
his hand moving
up and down
like an ax.

(The Magazine Vendor)

On the ferry

where he is not supposed
to sell, he flits
from seat to seat,
lounging nonchalantly
as a crew member passes,
then rises up
and chirps his sales,
fluttering orange magazines
at the tips
of his wings.

(The Tambourine Player)

He sits at night
at the back of the ferry,
black and thin,

drumming rhythm
into his fingers
while a group of men

gathers around him
chanting Africa
across dark water.

(The Madman)

His bushy hair,
his laughing beard,
his dancing pagan eyes
watch the ferry passengers

while he talks
to himself
(nodding his head)
of important
nothing.

(The Boat Guard)

Her dark brown face
the color of her uniform,
she stands lazy, bored,
her power
packed into a night stick.

(The Flower Carrier)

The pot of orchids
balanced on his head,
leafing high
—orange purple white
red—strange
cockscomb for
a bird of paradise.

(The Water Carrier)

Halfway up the hill
he pauses underneath a palm,
his two metal buckets
and wooden yoke
resting on green grass
while behind him
the bay
gleams bright blue.

(Teenage Schoolgirls)

All laughing, giggly,
wiggly in short skirts
above women's legs,
they lollipop
to their love boys.

(The Beggar with an Umbrella)

Brightly clothed
and carrying a red beach umbrella
like a parasol,
she approaches with her sharp
thin body
etched with black ink
into the blue day,
and holds out her hand
and asks if we
can arrange some change,
offhandedly,
like a friend.

(The Drummers)

At the back of the bus
seven men
beat out cuica,

panels, drums,
alive to the sun,
the blue sky,

rising hills
of rebellion
in the heart.

(The Country Couple)

The city
whistling their thin clothes,
the man dazed,
pale mustache
brushed dusty wheat,
and the woman,
pale eyes lost,
her back hooked
in a question mark.

(The Chief Clerk)

His gold face beaming
holiness,
he tells
how he bought
a hut on the hill
and will be
living in the
slums.

(The Servant Girl)

She calmly wheels the baby carriage
through the plaza in Ipanema,
proud mulata, erect, her delicate
features beautiful as a lady,
while her dumpy mistress flusters
around her like a satellite.

(The Hunchback Beggar)

Proud of his pain,
he sits on the sidewalk,
his bare chest twisted

to slap the eyes
of people walking by.

(The Accounting Clerk at Lunch)

Sitting
hooked over his desk,
his left hand
holds a sandwich,

his right
taps a samba
into American music
on the radio.

(The Consulate Guard)

Far from home,
hair clipped,
he guards
a lonely boy
in shining
red white black
uniform.

(The Street Vendor Selling Pens)

Four feet high,
his torso straight and strong,
his legs gnarled and strong
like the stump of an oak,
he stands, feet apart,
eyes challenging,
fist thrust forward
radiating pens between his fingers
like the blessing
of an ancient saint.

The Man with No Legs

The man with no legs
rides a black wooden box
with small steel wheels.
He moves with long arms
pushing the pavement.
His face is the face
of a dignitary;
his arms are the strong
arms of a chimpanzee.
Even taxi drivers
stop to let him cross,
braked in holy superstition.

The Crazy Woman
at the Ferry Dock

(Rio de Janeiro)

Thin. Hard bodied.
She faces the lines
of people, her eyes glazed,
fists clenched, mouth
shouting a tide of
curses.
   Suddenly
she stops. The air
stands still and hot.
The crowd waits,
then starts to taunt her,
lazily, to pass time.
She sweats, and then
her muscles tense,
her wild eyes
look into the people
and
   Oh Lord!
wring her like a rag
and out flows hate.

The Beggar Woman

(The Mosaic Sidewalks of Rio)

Her legs broken and deformed,
useless bones no bigger than a child's,
she crawls the street, her hands
pushing in front of her a small bag
and a tin pan half filled with cheap coins.

All who walk around her are giants.
Her brown, vulnerable eyes
look up from the bright, patterned sidewalk,
caught like a crippled dog
in its design.

Motor Scooter Girl

(Rio de Janeiro)

…beep, beep, beeping
the motor scooter boy
whisks, speeding
in thick traffic,

cars on each side
—a wrist twitch away
from crashing pain,
metal searing death—

his girl behind him
with blue helmet
but bare legs,
bare brown arms

clinging his waist,
trusting,
so easily
slashed, maimed,

killed—oh
my God, so
vulnerable.

The Dancers

Night: The Beach at Flexas

[to the music of *atabaque* drums,
 agogô bells, *xequerê* rattles]

Round black women
in full white dresses
swish to the motion

of sea white waves,
swirling left,
swirling right,

swirling once around
to the edge of the sea,
then back through sand

(- bare feet—
— rum bottles—
— candle light—)

Thin black men
stand aside,
clapping hands,

singing to the waves,
singing to the wind,
sea goddess

moon goddess
weaving white fingers
into black night.

Flower Sellers
along the Cemetery Wall

(São Paulo)

Gray morning.
The concrete street,
the sidewalk,
the cemetery wall,
the hazy air
above the wall,
are all gray.

Along the wall,
under colorless
tin roofs,

the flower sellers
in gray dresses
talk the day's news

while ORANGE
YELLOW PURPLE
burst
beside them.

Behind them,
over the wall,
loom gray angels
of dead stone.

Vespers

(Rio de Janeiro)

The walls of the church
at Largo de Misericordia
are white as the dress
of the Mãe de Santo
who dances to the drums
praising Oxalá.

The statues of the church
at Largo de Misericordia
are gold brown as the skin
of the young drummer
who beats out the rhythm
of the samba.

The altar of the church
at Largo de Misericordia
has lights that rise
seven levels, like lights
of the slum on the hill
behind Botafogo.

Oxalá: chief god of Condomblé and Macumba, Afro-Brazilian cults widely
practiced among the poor; Mãe de Santo: a priestess of those cults; Botafogo:
a middle class district of Rio.

IV

Rio de Janeiro, 1978-79

The Declining Days of the
Military Dictatorship

A Child, Dead in Chicago

(Rio de Janeiro—1978)

By telephone the news goes out,
networking the world on lines that vibrate
awed silence, a cough, a pause,
a helpless, "I'm so sorry."
                              In
twenty countries hundreds of men
stop for a moment, look at the walls
around them, and a great machine stumbles
for an instant to a halt.
                              By telex
at night the messages come in,
tapping sympathy into a dark, empty room.

The Office Sonnets

(Rio de Janeiro, 1978. A law office along the Avenida Rio Branco. The military dictatorship is in its 14th year; it will last seven more. For a decade resistance has found refuge and protection in the Church. Now union leaders, students, professionals, members of base Christian communities, begin to speak out. Tension hovers in the air. Street demonstrations are suppressed by heavily armed police.)

#1

We sit in our glass office and are bored,
the hours lounging by with typists' clatter;
we listen to the secretaries chatter
boy friends, week ends, weak longings as we store

our writing in gray cabinets. Oh Lord,
each sound outside we hope to see glass shatter,
hear shouts of freedom, watch bullets splatter
the fine wood paneling. Afterward

we close day, lock doors, head toward
the elevator, ride down, minds blurred
to another day's dream torn and tattered
to tears, despairing, as though tears mattered.

"Where is your peace, Jesus? Where is your sword?"
We step outside, night answers like a chord.

#2

Dark is the night that sets, and dark the soul,
but not so dark as in the night of day
where all fluorescent, paled and paled away,
the empty belfries toll and toll and toll.

"Here's your memorandum ready. Did you say
 something? I thought you did. Is something wrong?"
Girl, can't you hear the bells? They toll so long,
toll in empty belfries, tall, cold, gray

against the terrored night. "Ding dong, ding dong,"
like a child's rhyme losing all control
and crying through the dark, "He stole
a thief in the night, his voice sweet as song."

Dark is the night that sets, and dark the soul,
and the bells toll deep and sweet and strong.

Workmen Repairing the Flagpole
on the Municipal Hall

Rio de Janeiro, 1978
(during the military dictatorship)

1.

They stand elevated on its base,
three black men—one uniformed in green,
one in red & yellow, one in white & blue,

shining in sunlight, bright like figures
carved on a German public clock.

The flag pole wavers in their arms.

2.

Once this would have been heroic.
Once whole monarchies, regimes,
trembled to the muscles of workers
raising flags.
                        This morning,
people watch with mild curiosity.

3.

In 1785, the painter David
exhibited the Oath of the Horatii:
three brothers strong and proud.
Its political implications were
immediately apparent. He wrote
Jean Antoine Gros, "You love art
too well to concern yourself
with frivolous subjects."

Riot Troops on the Avenida Rio Branco

Rio de Janeiro, September 12, 1979
(the declining days of the Brazilian military dictatorship)

Slow moving, easy muscled giants stand,
thick clubs palmed in their hands like toys;
the lazy innocence of little boys
floats on their faces, sun blind tanned.

They are at ease. Their uniforms mark
tension on the crowd. The passing noise
of cars soars to a silent peak, poised
dangerously under the blazing arc

of blue sky. The people walking by
know without looking, and the why
of the people's silence penetrates the noise,
reaching up with a pierced, gagged voice
to lift and touch and—bleeding—
brand the fiery sky with mute demand.

"Look at the Women of Rio..."

(1978)

Look at the women of Rio: They have tired eyes
rimmed by sophisticated tan faces that tell lies

of fullness and leisure. Theirs is a city of play,
and play they do all night and work all day,

attend the university because its chic,
and chic to leave the kids with mom all week

and on the weekend mimic the social life
of mother, student, worker, lover, wife

wrapt all in one: Bronzed, baked, oldened by the sun,
they circulate nervous status, call it fun,

walking with studied smoothness on the beach.
High above, and far beyond their reach,

slum shacks cluttering the mountains, tossed
there by a giant hand, bright-painted, cruciformed in pain,
look down and pity the city that is empty, lost.

Rio de Janeiro. Carnaval.

(1978)

Say we are not in the colonies.
Pretend revolt. The rich
of Rio play the native elite
impeccably: soft, spoiled,
envious, fawning their masters
with swift, lazy hate.

A bright float sambas Coca Cola
down the Avenida Rio Branco. ·
There is some dispute
whether the best carnaval ball
is that sponsored
by Atlantic, Esso, or Shell.

V

Tropical Thoughts

September 5, 1969

(A Peace Corps Volunteer, stationed in Brazil,
reads of the death of Ho Chi Minh. September 7
is Brazilian Independence Day.)

Passing the post office, I return
to the small room. The Brazilian
blue sky shines above a day spent
translating a long and kindly
pineapple-ist from Del Monte,
interested in a canning plant.

What are these shapes that shade across
my room, but Gordon at Khartoum
and the tenuous comfort of
conquerors? Outside uniformed
schoolchildren pound drums and practice
marching for Independence Day.

Jefferson at Monticello;
around him lies Virginia, green
from the far hills (a thousand
misted memories). The heat sings,
a breeze wends up the orchard slope
to the mansion. He turns to write
a letter to the dying Adams.

Bright-Colored Birds

I

The parrots and the toucans in the park
seize bright pieces of popsicle
through the bars: orange, yellow, red—
seize them with black beaks,
taste them with black tongues, and throw
back their heads to swallow
the bright-colored popsicle pieces.

Orange, yellow, blue, green, red—
the toucans and the parrots circle
in the cage, crying, circle with strange
voices crying in the shade of the leaves
whose colors do not change.

II

And I have seen the pea-birds mating.
Slowly the peacock circles the great cage,
slowly he shows the colors of his great tail's
green eyes, slowly within the shadows
of the green leaves he cries;
in the green shadow of the leaves

I have seen the pea-hen waiting.
Quickly the peacock circles the cage,
quickly in the colors of his green tail's
great eyes, quickly in the sunlight between
shadows where the pea-hen trembles, waiting,
quickly she is caught in the swirling rage,
swirled in the colors, in the sunlight
shadows eyes lifted flying high
born—
            then   ending   dies.

Then the peacock rises up and
cries into the sunlight of lost skies.

III

The oldest parrot in the park
has blue head feathers that tremble
in the wind. His eyes are wise
and, when he speaks, his voice
is mellow with many memories.
At night, when things are dark
blue, I pass his cage and
often hear him singing.

Cantilena

The poor of São Paulo
say there is a secret train
in the Amazon jungle.

It glides silently
on narrow tracks
under arches of trees

so close no plane
can ever see it.
They say it carries

diamonds, uranium, gold,
and that the jungle
grows so green and tight

only birds see,
and jaguars, and
the dark eyes of Indians.

Sunday Afternoon:
The Country Club at Santa Cruz

The line of cattle at the top of the hill
moves solemnly to the samba beat.
The music is fast, the cattle are slow;
their massive shoulders, heaving, fill

the rhythm with a power more still
than men and women by the radio
dancing their fingers and hips and feet
to electric drums, while their lips spill

laughter as little and brittle and shrill
as clinking glasses where sugary sweet
liquor flows, tinkling treat, until
their eyes rise wide, look up and know
the hilltop and the things that go
slowly onward, forever, complete.

Poem in Black and White:
The Slums at Santo Amaro

(for Richard Collins Davis)

May we remember patterns in black and
white: shadows on dirt streets in morning light,
the bright sun torturing afternoon, and
the startling intimacy of night
pressed against naked plaster houses.

May we imagine that all patterns are
squared: neatly rectangular like flower beds
in the praça at Santo Amaro,
where we drank coffee with pale blondes
in an outdoor café. May we pretend
that the streets of Bairro Subaré
are careful lessons in geometry,
neatly laid out despite old men on doorsteps
spitting blood into the dust.

May we picture a white American moving
down dark skinned streets among dark eyes
that wait. May we suppose he knows the love,
the hate that pours out empty
as the sun rises, cutting white walls
with black shadow, and then, and only
then, senses something he cannot know,
fetid and breathing like an animal,
creeping unbelievably near.

Poem in Brown and Gray:
The Slums at Santo Amaro

On the jagged dirt paths
of Bairro Subaré,
where the houses stand close
and white plaster walls
sweat the smell of flesh,
a young white man with a beard
moves among brown skins,
respected and reserved,
asking quiet questions
and jotting down the answers,
about sewage, about rains,
about walls that breathe tuberculosis.

The reform candidate
sits in his office
and speaks with deep sincerity
to the quiet man with a beard
about the need for data,
a solid base for planning.
"You know the place," he says.
"They know you, trust you."
His eyes hold
brown visions of renewed lives.

The reform mayor
sits in his office
his eyes brown, sincere.
The man with a beard
holds a sheaf of papers
in his hand.
The reform mayor smiles;
his eyes hold visions.
Yes, yes, they're important.
Today he's busy.
Perhaps next week,
he says, and
the man with the beard
becomes an old man.

Brazilian Poem

When the bus
from São Rafael to São Gabriel
plunges off a cliff,
all passengers and the driver
being killed,
there will always be someone
who got on at the last stop
half a kilometer
before.

But then,
there will always be someone
who got off there
too.

Bobagem Poética

"If dogs are immortal, so is Brazil."
That's what the poet Charlie Itzen said.
I admit we never knew just what he meant,
except I remembered a dead dog, lying

on a mud street in Bairro São Benedito,
high on a hill above Vitória.

On the other hand, in Guatemala City
there's a statue that's dedicated:
"From Eternal Rome To Immortal Guatemala."
Around it the tawny city

circles restlessly, rising up
to scratch its fleas.

Hummingbirds in the Tropics

*"Writers have often lost their way trying to explain
how brilliant a jewel the hummingbird is."*
-Richard Hughes

Writers have often lost their way
between the beak and the description;
between the hot, silent afternoon
and the clean white page, they
have often lost their way.

        Held by the humming wings
        Yet still, stiller than the afternoon,
        Poised, the sun sparkling on the
        Deep blue bodyfeathers, the long beak
        Poised, approaching the flower, slowly,
        Perfectly, the long tail feathers
                Deep green.

A mass of brilliant blossoms and no
leaves, hidden in a swarm of hummingbirds
so vivid as to far outshine the flowers.
Between the beak touching the flower
and the description lies the page;
the tropics were not made to be written.

        Deep green like the damp forest
        When the bright sun shines through it
        In afternoon, deep blue and sparkling,
        Still except for the wings that hum
        So fast they seem still, and the long
        Thin beak touching the flower.

Dom João Fonseca, up from Vitoria bay,
wandering in the forest, saw a jewel—
blue as a pool, green as the forest,
still, yet quick beyond description.
He followed it and lost his way.

Tropical Thoughts

"Then in every way such prisoners would deem reality
to be nothing else than the shadows of the artificial objects."
-Plato, The Republic

1.

From the chair in which he sat, he could see
the television screen, and in the television screen
(the television being off)
he could see the reflection of an open window.
Out the open window was a patch of sky:
blue, with small clouds (the clouds and sky
mirrored gray-green). Across the sky flew a bird.

2.

An old man walking in the street,
his feet bare, his ankles swollen, sored,
his forehead sweating beneath kinked gray
hair. Black skin shows through the tears
in his clothes; the smile on his face

is also a tear.

A boy running to a closed door,
his arms thin, his belly bulged and tight.
He knocks loudly into an empty house;
"Dona! Dona!" he shouts, and once more
"Dona!" Then everything is quiet

as before.

3.

He did not see, but he did not need to see.

He saw a bird pass in the television screen.
The clouds behind the bird increased.
Silence hung in the air like humidity.

Somewhere in jungles a parrot did not scream.

The tropics are a threat that never happens.

VI

Dry Lands

The Brazilian Northeast

Poem Beginning with a Line from Garcia Lorca

(for Bairro Boa Vista)

There are souls that have
bright roofs of red tile
so sun shows through, orange

like a child's hand held
close to the lamp, fingers
together, so the flesh glows
and the bones stand out
in black strong lines; there

are souls that have windows
that open wide, without glass
or screens, and look over sky
bright blue as a child's
dream when the lamp's turned

down and the night stands
black starred beyond
the kerosene's faint flicker.

A Farmhouse, a Tree

-the dry interior of Northeastern Brazil
("The Juazeiro Tree Has Deep Roots...")

Everything's brown: the land is dust,
the mountains dust, the trees and
the sky the color of dust. Except
for a white house and the bright slash
of a magenta bush,
and one tree, startling green.

What is this tree that in this
land of rust and rush-
ing winds, stands (in the
setting sun) a memory of lush
Illinois springs, so startling green?

Twisted Trees

(the Brazilian dry lands)

All afternoon the dry wind
pierces the blank sun-tortured land
where nothing grows but runted, bleached trees,
twisted like the sheets on a fever bed.

I am thinking of old fevers:
the white sun pierces my brain.
Slowly I remember a thin white hand
reaching toward an empty glass of water.

All night long I had lain
and dreamt of a land like this,
populated by waterless winds,
tall bleached bones and twisted trees.

Three Metaphors

(A Brazilian prairie town)

1.

Restless like a traveller,
he hurries to where there is no station
and no train waiting,
carrying pride like a suitcase.

2.

He walks where she cannot see him,
a lone gunfighter in a silent town,
waiting for his enemies.

3.

Stars stand above a single tree.
Far across the blackened city
comes the silence of a dog barking.

Linhares, 1969

(a Brazilian prairie sawmill town at dawn)

I arrive with the morning.
The roosters greet me like trumpeters,
calling out across the city and
echoing. Far down a brick street
mist hangs lightly between the pinpoints
of streetlamps still burning.

I am reminded of
a print of 19th century Chicago:
the brick and wide dirt streets wake up
to the whirr of commerce; the loading
and unloading, the shouts, the men of
industry. High above

the prairie clouds are churning:
there will be an afternoon thunderstorm.
It will strike fiercely and clear quickly,
leaving the city at night quiet and
starlit and pierced by the flash and whine
of sawmill wheels turning.

Zebú at Dusk

Three small dogs, black and white,
Bark at the heels of a Brahma bull
- Big and tender, white and full.
Bark to the day. Bark to the night.

Call the Brahma bull Zebú
- Big Zebú with the brown doe's eye -
Runs away like a cloud in the sky
- The late day sky, deep dark blue.

Runs in the dusty streets of the town
- Dust from his heels in the golden light -
Runs by the church that is dog hide white
- Barking its bells as the sun goes down.

Quiet comes with the dying light.
Stillness comes when the moon is full.
White, now silent, Brahma bull
Gleams of the day. Gleams in the night.

Moon Glows above an Alagoas Hill...

Moon glows above an Alagoas hill,
Light white moon in the afternoon of day,
Pale moon on the pale blue sky
Above the grass that is pale green gray.

Bus rides on the flat gray road,
Climbs the hill with wheeze and sway;
Yellow bus with a golden strip,
Dirty with mud of blood red clay.

What is the ghost that haunts this hill?
Black slave falls on his knees to pray.
Behind him he hears the dog on his trail;
Man with a gun hunts runaway.

Bus breaks the hovering peace of time,
Shatters the haunting stillness of day;
Wrenches a scream from the pale sky,
Forces the pain, one instant, away.

VII

Rivers

The Brazilian Amazon

Look, I Tell My Daughters...

1.

Look, I tell my daughters; look
and remember. Night darkening
over a palm-thatched mud-brick house,
a wooden door opened to the night, and,
on a rough wooden table, a candle
casting light onto the dirt floor.

A horse tethered outside the door.

You will not see these things
much longer.

2.

    A cowhand
in brown leather, his strong
weathered hand guiding the reins
of his brown stallion, lifting
a cattle horn to his lips,
blowing the loud, low sound
that guides the small herd
through the dusty streets
of the town.

In Praise of Places without Electricity

(Brazil: The Araguaia River)

The woman stands in the open door.
Late glowing twilight flows in,
faintly luminating the room's dusk,
touching the cool brick floor,
the worn wooden table, the woman's
print dress, brown arms and hands,
her dark graying hair, her face
laced with lines and peaceful,
dark eyes gazing deep and thought filled
toward the wide, slow river.

Dona Josefa: 1910-1986

(in a Brazilian frontier village)

Your broad, half-Indian face dignified
in death—a nut brown carved face,
wrapped in cheap white, a trimming of blue lace:
surely you make, for Christ, a treasured bride.

Last Palm Sunday we watched your wide
bottle-shaped body waddle to your place
(much loved) in our dusty church: you graced
that day with a giant fan-shaped palm,

your sharp quick humor and your heart-deep calm.
And five days later, the day Christ died
again in our village play, you walked beside
our village actors, the long, long mile of prayer:
and you were fully with us, and yet truly <u>there</u>,
and held each of us in your heart, and cried.

Praying for the Dead:
The Cemetery at Caseara

*(anniversary of the death of
Adão Pereira de Souza,
born 1944, murdered 1988)*

The words are words like any words:
to his mother, his wife, his daughter,
weeping their year-old grief—blurred
to endless sound like running water

comfortingly heard and yet unheard.
But still the words are strong,
true and precise, real as breeze-stirred
candle flames over the grave, as long

shadows cast by afternoon sun on hard,
barren ground. Listen our eyes upward:
a brown-eyed young man, no relative,
standing back by one of the stunted trees
that mark our cemetery with short lives,
lifts up his head suddenly, and sees.

Father Josimo Tavares:

(murdered at Imperatriz, Brazil
May 10, 1986)

"Get the black priest," they said,
leaning against the pickup truck,
the small white car, bellies bulging over
their holster belts. All their hate
was balled up in that small dark figure
standing between them and land they lusted,
lean arms stretched against the sky.

"Get the black priest." So,
in the quiet of Saturday afternoon
as he climbed the long stairs
of the nearly empty building,
two shots roared out
and all his people's fears
began to fall.

Justice in Goiás

Senhor Josias and his family
had been farming the land fourteen years
when the State Secretary of Police arrived
and told them that they and their neighbors
were invaders, law breakers
—that he could bring a truckload
of police with machine guns,
so they'd better sign
                              (that same day
the court issued a decree granting
Senhor Josias and his neighbors
rights to the land; the court officer
started out on the four hour trip
from the county seat)
                              and they herded
Senhor Josias and his family
and their neighbors into town
where the police said, "Sign here."
"Why?" asked Senhor Josias, and
they said, "Because our boss said so..."

(and the court officer crossed
the Caipó River on his way)

and Senhor Josias' wife said,
"Sign, Josias"—it had been
a long struggle, their house burnt down
three times, gunmen haunting the land,
beatings, death threats.
                              "Why?"
asked Senhor Josias, and she looked at him
with the look that said his life
was worth more than land
                              (and
the court officer reached the edge
of town)
                              and his neighbors were

brought in one by one and signed,
and they were scared
                    (the court officer
reached the police station and,
finding out what was going on,
strolled up and down the street,
waiting)
            and when the last had signed,
Senhor Josias, tired, the police and
gunmen watching, reached over and
picked up the pen.

A Meeting In Goiás

One by one the men and women rise
to tell their stories: simple men,
lined from squinting against sunlight,
hands hard and large from working land;

women with dark faces and tired eyes
that have watched children die. One by one
the stories are told: gunmen moving in,
houses burned, beatings, a child thrown

against the rocks, a neighbor gunned down
in the night. One by one they tell
of leaving land, of rich ranchers bringing
in cattle as the people huddle

in landless shacks and see their children
slowly starve. One by one, in the silence,
after the telling, they stand ill-at-ease
before the listeners, and shift

from foot to foot, dark eyes questioning,
waiting for something to be done.

VII

Wednesday Morning

Late Afternoon, Itacajá

Rain water beads the barbed wire fence,
turns the sagging, rusted wires silver
in late afternoon sun. A spider has spun
her web between the top wire and the next.

The sun in the west, pale yellow, flares
below gray clouds. The last dripping
rain-drops fall with a clip-clipping
sound on dead leaves; a tree raises bare

arms against the sky. Here is the text:
the day, the rain, over and done—
the beads of rainwater on wire quiver
in twilight air—clean, gray, intense.

Poem Beginning with a Line from Our Daughter's English Composition

"Now Brazil is raining light and hard."
The strange, musical phrase of our daughter's
words, catching afternoon sunlight that slants
under great slate clouds moving toward

us from the east, the swift forward
pitching wind, the trembling green of new plants
in the garden, the way falling water
starts quick and fine, each drop starred

in sunlight, then suddenly bursts downward
brutally
                 —all caught between sun and rain
as her ten year old mind is caught in
two countries, two languages, memories scattered
and (like a fine vase, wind blown) shattered
in gleaming pieces, deep light in each shard.

A Road in Espírito Santo

(for my wife)

That rainy mountain night:
we rounded a hill—
a huge Mercedes truck
in our lane moved toward us,
its three-point logo clenched
in the gritting teeth of its grill—
drenched pavement, dazzling confusion
of lights. I spun the wheel
to the right where the shoulder
lay soft mud above a black chasm.

If we had died? We'd
have left aside worries, pains,
arguments—love, longing, moments
of great wonder...

                  I think of it
fourteen years later,
you riding here beside me:
how in that mountain bend
we left part of our lives,
how, when it comes right down to it,
all of us are risen from the dead.

Ode on St. Cecilia's Day

São Paulo. Rush hour. A rainy night.
Cars struggle along the Avenida São João
- headlights glancing raindrops down
red tail lights, glowing bright

in starts and stops; horns,
motors, shouts, wheels, rain
swishing streets in soft refrain
of singing, swiftly sensed—torn

from our hearing and sharply borne
in wet wind, upward:

The Church of St. Cecilia's tower
soaring in soot dirty sky -
dwarfed, yet not dwarfed by
tall buildings. Light of a door

cracked open; song of a choir
from inside whispering streetward -
drowned, then heard, then drowned
by passing noise, rising higher

- skyward—the night afire
suddenly in sound:

a saint's soft voice, sworn
silently in the reeling dark.
A child born.

"Wednesday Morning. The Widows Come from Mass..."

Wednesday morning. The widows come from mass
walking together in plain, black dresses.
A gray memory of rain caresses
their lips. Trees whisper as they pass.

What is their love that year after year
they choose to meet the morning dressed in black?
Live! their daughters cry. But they turn back
smiling to life, untouched by the fear

that puts on bright clothes and dances wild
in the night. All the world is a child
to their eyes: loved, amusing, quick to pass,
yet captured in quiet mornings where the will
sweeps breathtaking upward while hours stand still,
clean and lovely, silent and clear as glass.

Acknowledgments

"In Praise of Places without Electricity" appeared in *Allegro*.

"A Road in Espírito Santo" appeared in *America*.

"Finding" appeared in *The Apple Valley Review*, and was nominated for a Pushcart Prize and Best New Poets.

"Sunday Afternoon: The Country Club at Santa Cruz" appeared in *Assisi*

"A Farmhouse, a Tree..." appeared in *The Chicago Tribune Magazine*.

"In the Village of São Lourenço: Portrait with Distant Landscape" appeared in *The Christian Poetry Review*.

"Block Houses" and "Ode on St. Cecilia's Day" appeared in *Dappled Things*.

"A Child, Dead in Chicago" appeared in *Fuel*.

"Rio de Janeiro. Carnaval," "Brazilian Poem," and "Father Josimo Tavares" first appeared in *Longhouse*. "Rio de Janeiro. Carnaval," subsequently appeared in *Fuel* and in *The Shimer College Symposium*.

"Sketches/Rio de Janeiro," "The Crazy Woman at the Ferry," "The Man with no Legs," "The Beggar Woman," and "Working Men Repairing the Flagpole on the Municipal Hall" appeared in *Hotmetalpress*.

"Linhares," "Look, I Tell My Daughters," "Three Metaphors," "Twisted Trees," & "Vespers" appeared in *Indiana Voices*.

"Bobagem Poética" appeared in *The Main Street Rag*.

"Moon Glows above an Alagoas Hill...." appeared in *The New Laurel Review*.

"Dona Josefa" and "Caseara Cemetary" appeared in *New Song*.

"Like White Swans Swimming, The Tropical Nuns...." appeared in *Open Places*.

"Angelica at 10 Years of Age" and "Angelica in the Tropics" appeared in *Papyrus*.

"Ana Cristina in Her Fourth Year" and "Poem Beginning with a Line from My Daughter's English Composition" appeared in *Plains Poetry Journal*. "Ana Cristina in Her Fourth Year" also appeared in *The Christian Poetry Review* and was commended in the 2008 Margaret Reid Poetry Contest.

"Cantilena" appeared in *Potpourri*.

"Poem in Black and White" appeared in *Rattapallax*.

"A Meeting in Goiás" and "Justice in Goiás" appeared in *The Roanoke Review*.

"Wednesday Morning, The Widows Come from Mass..." appeared in *The Semi-Dwarf Review*.

"A Mulata Child on the Itaipu Bus" first appeared in *Sisters Today* and subsequently in *Manna* and *The Shimer College Symposium*.

"Jardim Zoológio" appeared in *The South Carolina Review*.

"September 5, 1969" and "Bright-Colored Birds" appeared in *The Southern Poetry Review*.

"Poem Beginning with a Line from Garcia Lorca" appeared in *The Southwest Review*.

"In the Village of São Lourenço: May, the Month of the Virgin," "Hummingbirds in the Tropics," "Poem in a White Room with a Window," and "Zebu at Dusk" appeared in *Sou'wester*.

"Riot Troops on the Avenida Rio Branco" appeared in *Windhover*.

Arthur **Powers** went to Brazil in 1969 and lived there most his adult life. He and his wife, Brenda, spent seven years in the eastern Amazon, organizing subsistence farmers. They also lived in Rio de Janeiro, Recife, Bahia, Minas Gerais, and Espírito Santo.

Arthur is the recipient of A Fellowship in Fiction from the Massachusetts Artists Foundation, the 2012 Tuscany Novella Prize, the 2014 Catholic Arts & Letters Award, and numerous other literary honors. His poetry has appeared in *America, Chicago Tribune Magazine, Dappled Things, Hiram Poetry Review, Roanoke Review, South Carolina Review, Southern Poetry Review, Sou'wester, Windhover,* & many other magazines & anthologies.

www.ingramcontent.com/pod-product-compliance
Lightning Source LLC
Chambersburg PA
CBHW031043110426
42740CB00048B/1049